8751

NOTES FROM THE
UNSTRUCK MUSIC

from

THE GĀYAN

of

INAYAT KHAN

Message Publications
Tucson, Arizona, U.S.A.

For information please write
Munira van Voorst van Beest
    34, Rue de la Tuilerie
    92150 Suresnes, France.

or
Message Publications
    P.O. Box 40275
    Tucson, Arizona 85717
    U.S.A

Distributed to the trade by:

Omega Press
RD 1 Box 1030E
New Lebanon, NY 12125

ISBN 0-930872-34-7

PREFACE

This new edition of *Notes from the Unstruck Music from The Gāyan of Inayat Khan* has been prepared from the source materials published in *Authentic Versions of the Teachings of Pir-o-Murshid Inayat Khan on Sufism: Sayings, Part I* (London and The Hague; East-West Publications, 1982). The guideline followed in preparing this edition has been to give the Pir-o-Murshid's own text for the *Gāyan*: the sayings from his notebooks as dictated by him (often with alterations) for this purpose, and his own classification of the sayings, arranged by him in accordance with the whole atmosphere of each saying. Consequently, most of the changes introduced by the mureeds (followers) entrusted with the task of assisting in the preparation of the *Gāyan* for publication have not been retained here (except where the English seemed absolutely to require them). These changes have naturally appeared in all subsequent editions of the *Gāyan*, since no earlier texts were available until the publication of *Authentic Versions* in 1982. The changes were typical of the approach and understanding of the 'twenties, when the *Gāyan* was originally compiled. Today—more than sixty years later—there is a renewed interest in the original words and texts of Pir-o-Murshid Inayat Khan's teaching. Those who have long been familiar with the *Gāyan* as published up to now will probably continue to prefer the sayings in the form and under the classification to which they have become accustomed. This edition is not intended to replace those earlier editions, but to make the original inspiration of Pir-o-Murshid Inayat Khan available in a form more readily accessible than that of the *Authentic Versions*. For the categories of classification (*Alapa*s, *Alankara*s, etc.) Pir-o-Murshid Inayat Khan's own indications have here been restored, rather than the extensive reclassifications by those who prepared the book. This frequently changes the sequence of the sayings. For example, under *"Sura"* are placed first those sayings classified by Pir-o-Murshid as *Sura*s and previously published as such; then follow all sayings classified by Pir-o-Murshid as *Sura*s but previously published under some other category. Certain sentences from lectures given by Pir-o-Murshid Inayat Khan, added to the *Gāyan* as sayings, have been included here only if their classification came from the Pir-o-Murshid himself.

Suresnes, 1985
Munira van Voorst van Beest
Munir Graham

TERMS USED IN THE VARIOUS
CLASSIFICATIONS OF GĀYAN

Alapa. — God speaking to man.
This is the principal theme of the Message.

Raga. — The human soul calling upon the beloved God.

Sura. — God speaking through the kindled soul.

Tala. — The rhythmic expression of an idea.

Bola. — A kindled word.

Tana. — The soul speaking with Nature.

Chala. — An illuminated word.

Alankara. — The fanciful expression of an idea.

Gamaka. — The feeling of a poet's heart, keyed to various notes.

Gayatri. — Prayers.

ALAPAS.

When a glimpse of Our image is caught in man,
When the heaven and the earth are sought in man,
Then what is in the world that is not in man?
If one only explored him there's a lot in man.

If you will go forward to find Us,
We will come forward to receive you.

Give up all you have, and We shall give
you all We possess.

In man We have designed Our image,
in woman We have finished it.

In man We have shown Our nature benign;
in woman We have expressed Our art divine.

O peace-maker, before trying to make peace
throughout the world, make peace within thyself.

Thou art the master of life here and in
the hereafter.

ALANKARAS.

Indifference,
my most intimate friend,
I am sorry, for I always have to act as thy opponent.

My modesty,
thou art the thin veil that covereth subtle vanity.
My humility,
thou art the very essence of vanity.

Vanity,
both saint and sinner drink from thy cup.

Vanity,
Thou art the fountain of wine on the earth,
where cometh the King of heavens to drink.

Peacock,
is it not thy vanity which causeth thee to dance?

My bare feet,
step gently on the path of life, lest the thorns
which are lying on thy way will murmur
being trampled upon by you.

My ideal,
I imagine at moments as if we were playing see-saw;
when I rise up, thou goest down below my feet,
and when I go down, thou risest over my head.

8

Self-dependence,
thou makest me poor, but rich at the same time.

Wert thou not laughing under thy sleeves,
my beloved ideal,
when I was searching for thee on the earth?

My feeling heart,
I so often wish you were made of a rock.

My limitation,
thou art as a moth in the eye of my soul.

Money,
thou art a bliss and a curse at the same time.
Thou turnest friends into foes and foes into friends.
Thou takest away and givest at the same time
anxiety in life.

We are the apsaras of heaven,
when the wind plays music we dance.
Earthly treasure is not our seeking,
our reward is Indra's one glance.

Time,
I have never seen thee, but I have heard thy steps.

Time,
in my sorrow thou creepest, in my joy thou runnest,
in the hours of my patient waiting thou standest still.

Time,
thou are the ocean,
and every moment of life is thy wave.

Sky,
thou art a sea wherein my imagination's boat sails.

My thoughtful self,
reproach no one;
hold grudge against no one;
take revenge with no one;
bear malice against no one;
be wise.

Be kind to all;
tolerant to all;
considerate to all;
polite to all,
oh my thoughtful self.

My independent spirit,
how many sacrifices I make for thy maintenance,
and yet thou are never satisfied.

My simple trust,
how often thou hast failed me.
I still go on following you with my eyes closed.

BOLAS.

The whole life's good deeds may be drowned in the
flood caused by one single sin.

A wise man without willpower
is as a head without body.

All that one holds is conserved,
all that one lets go is dispersed.

Pure conscience gives the strength of a lion,
and by a guilty conscience
even a lion turns into a rabbit.

The only condition of life is making
one's own nature.

Be true or false, for you cannot be both.

The Truth is a divine inheritance found in the depth
of the heart of every man.

A life-long time is not sufficient to learn how to live
in this world.

In poverty all evils breed.

Reason is the illusion of reality.

Lull the devil to sleep.

It is not the action in itself that is sin or virtue,
it is the condition which makes it either one or the other.

The reality itself is its evidence.

You cannot prove to be what in reality you are not.

You must not try to be what in reality you are not.

Pleasure blocks,
but pain clears the way of inspiration.

The mystic does not wait till the hereafter, but does
all he can to progress just now.

Power demands subjection,
but if you cannot fight the power,
win it by surrender.

Human personality is a music which has a tone and
rhythm of its own.

Take oneself to task
instead of putting faults on others.

Human heart is the shell
in which sincerity as pearl is formed.

Love guides its own way.

Man makes his reasons to suit himself.

Singlemindedness ensures success.

Love of form progressing
culminates in love of the formless.

A worldly loss often turns into a spiritual gain.

The ideal is a means, but its breaking is the goal.

Many feel, but few think;
and fewer there are who can express their thought.

The value of sacrifice is in willingness.

Refined manners with sincerity make a living art.

Longing for vengeance is like a craving for poison.

God is the central theme of the poet.
God is the portrait which the prophet paints.

True belief is independent of reason.

The more a man knows, the more he finds there is
to learn.

When a soul is attuned,
its every action becomes a music.

Death is a tax that the soul has to pay for having had
a name and a form.

The best way of living is to live a natural life.

To justify self for wrong-doing on the ground that another is guilty of the same fault is far from just.

Do not take the example of another as an excuse for your wrong-doings.

All the situations of life are tests to distinguish between the real and the false.

If you wish to follow the path of saints,
first learn forgiveness.

Spare words if you wish your words to be powerful.

The gardener uses both roses in the flowerbed and thorns in making fences.

Love's best expression is indifference.

The unsociable person is a burden to the society.

Divinity is human perfection and divine limitation.

The wise show their admiration by respect.

Many admit the truth to themselves,
but few confess it to others.

It is the twist of thought that is the curl of the Beloved.

14

Satan comes in most beautiful garbs
to cover from the sight of man his highest ideal.

Behind is one spirit and one life;
how can we then be happy if our neighbours are not?

Nothing in the world is more valuable than every
moment of your life.

Self-pity is the cause of all the grievances of life.

A gift of love is priceless.

It is our perception of time which passeth,
time does not pass; time is God, and God is eternal.

The mystic begins by wondering at life.

The life of the mystic is a phenomenon
at every moment.

In beauty is the secret of divinity.
Clean body reflects purity of the soul.
It is the purity of soul which gives a tendency to cleanliness.
Cleanliness is the secret of health.
Clean body signifies clean mind.
Purity of the soul is reflected in the cleanliness of body.
It is the pure in spirit who keep their body clean.

Reserve gives weight to the personality.

A serious and yet pleasant-spoken man
is really honourable.

When soberness comes after the intoxication of life,
one begins to wonder.

A life with a foolish companion is worse than death.

The pain of life is a price paid for the quickening
of the heart.

By the power of endurance things become precious
and men become great.

The heart closed to man
means the heart closed to God.

Spirituality is the tuning of the heart;
neither by study nor by piety can one attain it.

A person's morals must be judged from his attitude
rather than from his action.

Reason is a flower with a thousand petals,
one covered by another.

Fighting against nature is rising above nature.

Simplicity of nature is the sign of saints.

Life is full of blessings
if one only knew how to have them.

Nothing false will succeed, and if it apparently succeeds it must only bring false benefit.

All that produces longing in the heart
deprives the heart of its freedom.

It is the exaltation of the spirit which is productive
of all beauty.

One virtue can take a stand against a thousand vices.

Consideration is born in the heart and is developed
in the head.

Life is distinguished by the pair of opposites.

There is nothing in this life's fair that we shall take
and will not have to pay for.

A diamond must be cut before its light can shine out.

Beyond goodness is trueness,
which is a divine quality.

Guilty conscience robs the will of its power.

The answer that uproots the question from its ground
is the answer of the truly inspired one.

His trust in others is of no value who has no trust
in himself.

Love develops into harmony,
and in harmony is born beauty.

Devotion is proved by sacrifice.

In nature it is God Who by the hand of man designs
and carries out His intended plans.

The word which is not heard is lost.

Consideration is the sign of the wise.

Man's attitude is manifest in the expression
of his countenance.

Sin is the fuel for virtue's fire.

The first lesson that the seeker after truth must
learn is to be true to oneself.

Subtlety is the art of intelligence.

People build four walls around their ideas,
lest their ideas may escape their imprisonment.

Love rises in emotion and falls in passion.

The whole trend of life is a journey from imperfection
to perfection.

Every soul has his own way in life;
if you walk another's way, you must borrow his eyes.

Man's personality reflects his thought and deed.

Reason is learned from the everchanging world,
but knowledge comes from the essence of life.

The domain of the mystic is his self over which he
is king.

If a person would become straightforward,
certainly a straight way would be opened before him.

No one can be human and not make a mistake.

Humility of conscience dims the radiance
of the countenance.

The desire to develop one's personality
is the real purpose of human life.

Man expresses his soul in every thing he does.

When the heart breaks, it gives birth to the soul.

There is no better companion than solitude.

Life is what it is; you cannot change it but you can
change yourself.

The word is living but the silence is life.

Who keeps no secrets has no depth in his heart.

19

The heart that cannot keep secret is like a vessel upside down.

Wisdom is attained in solitude.

There is no desire in the world which has no answer. If this philosophy were wrong, the creation would not exist.

If in Truth we shall not build our hope,
in what shall we build?

The admirer of nature is the true worshipper of God.

Love that depends not on reciprocity stands upon its own feet.

Patient endurance is the strongest means of defence.

All that is really worth while is difficult to attain.

It is not the situation in life, but it is man's attitude towards life that makes happy or unhappy.

Gain by the loss of another is not profitable in the end.

Talking wisdom is much easier than living it.

Charity is the expansion of the heart.

God is the answer to every question.

Make ye God a reality,
and God will make you the truth.

God made man, and man made good or bad.

Give all you have and take all you are given.

The Creator is lost in His own creation.

Natural Religion is the religion of Beauty.

All surrender to beauty willingly
and to power unwillingly.

The creation is not only the nature of God
but also His art.

Vanity is the impetus hidden
behind almost every impulse.

Vanity brings out the best and worst in man.

Time and space are but the divisions of the infinite.

Vanity is the sum total of every living activity
in the world.

A charming personality is gold with perfume.

A dancing soul expresses its rapture
through all its expressions.

A beautiful personality is as a beautiful piece of art
with life in it.

The Holy Mother was the stepping-stone for Jesus
toward Christhood.

Mahomet's sword was the charm of his personality.

When the personality of an artist is absorbed in his
art it becomes art itself.

Vanity is the mask over the object
that draws every soul.

Vanity is the crown of beauty and modesty
is its throne.

Nature is the very being of man;
therefore, he feels at one with nature.

In the country you can see God's glory
and in the city you can glorify His name.

The true art does not take man away from nature;
on the contrary, it brings him closer to it.

Man without character is
as a flower without perfume.

Love is a net in which hearts are caught as fishes.

22

While everyone in the world asks 'Why?' of his neighbour, the mystic asks this question of himself.

Man is pulled from four sides in life: by the ideal, nature, circumstances and law.

A child born on earth is an exile from heaven.

No tie can bind if your heart is free.

Great personalities are few and fewer still are those who can recognize and appreciate them.

No person living on earth can come up to your ideal except a hero from a story of the past.

The one whom you expect to be your ideal will prove to be your ideal someday when he has gone past.

The true ego is born of the ashes of the false ego.

If by accident you step in the mud, it is not necessary therefore to keep on the muddy path.

Matter is a state of the spirit.

A living word is life itself.

Sympathy breaks the congestion of the heart.

The action is the reaction of thought.

Reason is the master of the unbeliever and the slave of the believer.

When desire abides in a steady thought
it ensures success.

No sacrifice is ever too great to be offered to the cause of liberty.

The fruitless life is a useless life.

Gold is that which proves to be real to the end
of the test.

To make God intelligible, you have to make a God.

Truth alone can succeed falsehood and falsehood is the waste of time and loss of energy.

What begins with deception continues in it and ends in the same.

The wise says in one word what the foolish cannot explain in a thousand words.

Burning words rise from a glowing heart.

His own attitude becomes an obstacle on the path of the pessimist.

The shortage of patience starves virtue to death.

The seeming death is the real birth of the soul.

Truth that disturbs peace and harmony
is worse than a lie.

It takes a thousand lies to prove one false statement true,
and yet in the end it must prove false.

The way of the Sufi is to experience life
and yet to keep above it.

Live in the world but do not become of it.

Life is opportunity, not only to accomplish what one
desires, but even to fulfill what one's soul yearns for.

Nobleness of character is an inborn quality
as fragrance in the flower;
it cannot be taught or learnt.

One word of the truly inspired one answers a hundred
questions and avoids a thousand unnecessary words
of explanation.

Every moment of life is an opportunity
and the greatest opportunity
is to know the value of opportunity.

It is the spirit of discipleship which opens the vision.

You must find your ideal in yourself.
If no one comes up to your ideal, you must make one.

Nobody in the world can prove to be your ideal
unless you yourself make one.

Through matter the soul attains
to its highest realization.

If a desire is not fulfilled that means the person did
not know how to desire.

Failure is caused by indistinctness of motive.

The charming personality of the prophet is a divine
net in which God captures the souls drifting in
the world.

A clever person with a biting tongue is like a serpent
with its poisonous teeth.

We each create our God, but His form, not His life.

We each picture God in the form we imagine,
thus making many gods out of the one single Being.

God alone exists, as many gods or as one God,
for two means only twice one.

CHALAS.

The spiritual guide performs the role of Cupid
in bringing the seeking souls closer to God.

The same light which is fire on earth and the sun in
the sky, is God in heaven.

It is presumption on the part of man when he demands
in words an explanation of God.

Beauty which modesty covers, art discovers gently;
while respecting human tendency, it unveils beauty
which human convention hides.

God lives in nature and is buried alive under the
artificial forms which stand covering Him
as His graves.

The good reputation is as fragile as a glass.

The good reputation is a trust given to man from
people, and it is the sacred duty of man to prove
worthy of this trust.

Take great care of your reputation,
if you at all care for it.

The man who has no reputation has no feeling
for the reputation of another.

Every person inherits from his ancestors
not only his body, but his mind also.

The wretched look for some excuse to be miserable.

You must never make fun with a fool; if you will
throw a flower at him in fun he will throw
at you a stone.

The alchemy is in the stilling of the heart,
when mercury becomes silver.

A real success is proved by its durability.

Stand through life as firm as a rock in the sea,
undisturbed and unmoved by its ever-rising waves.

Discovering of error is uncovering of light.

The truth spoken sincerely
certainly must carve the heart.

Spiritual attainment is the true purpose of every soul.

The more people you can get on with,
the wiser man you are.

Do you wish for a relief in life?
Rise above complexity and conventionality.

It does not matter what you have lost, so long as
your soul is not lost.

One single moment of truthful life is worth more than a thousand years of a life in falsehood.

Success gives a real appearance even to false things.

Worrying about the faults of others is an extra worry in addition to the worry that comes from one's own faults.

No one can sustain inharmony in life, though many ignorantly maintain it.

All things in their beginnings must be guarded from the sweeping wind of destruction, as the small plants must be nurtured in a glass house.

It is the ignorant believer who causes a revolt in an intelligent person by his claim of belief, thereby turning him into an unbeliever.

A selfish person cannot imagine anyone being unselfish.

The selfish always suspects the unselfish of falsehood.

God's majesty is seen in nature, but His scantiness in the grandeur of human life.

It takes but a moment to drop down from heaven to the earth, but to rise from the earth to heaven, even a lifetime would be insufficient.

If you walk through light and yet seek the path of darkness, it is like being pulled by the two poles of the world; you are torn between the two, neither can you go one way nor the other.

Joy and sorrow both are for each other; if it were not for joy, sorrow would not be; and if it were not for sorrow, joy would not be experienced.

Man wonders about his past and future; how wonderful would life become for him if he only realized the eternal now.

The spirit of discipleship is most necessary in one's journey along the spiritual path.

When it is so very difficult to prove truth to be true, how much more difficult must it be to prove true that which is false.

Purgatory is a state which mind experiences between the birth of thought and its materialization.

It is the darkness of your own heart which, falling on the heart of another, becomes a doubt in him.

Truth conceived by the mature soul is expressed as wisdom.

Goodness and wickedness both exist in human nature, only the difference is,

when one is manifest to view,
the other is hidden like a lining inside the coat.

The physical body is a necessity for the fulfilment
of the purpose of the soul.

Absence of generosity means that the doors
of the heart are closed.

Passing through an evolution on earth is necessary
for the spirit to arrive at its culmination.

A sarcastic remark can be more hurtful
than a scorpion's sting.

Let not your reputation fall in the hands
of the monkeys; they will look at it curiously,
mock at it, laugh at it, and snatch it
from each other's hands.
In the end they will tear it to pieces.

Do not entrust the devil with your secrets;
if you do so, then he who is meant to be your slave
will become your master.

With goodwill and trust in God, with self-confidence
and a hopeful attitude in life, a man will always win
his battle, however difficult.

All things existing have their opposites, save God.
It is therefore that God cannot be made intelligible
to the unbeliever.

31

Truth is purifying, truth is most lovable,
truth is peace-giving, but what is truth?
Truth is what you cannot speak.

If your fellowman does not pay you his debt, forbear
patiently; some day it will be paid back to you
to every farthing, together with its interest.

Heaven and hell are the material manifestation
of agreeable or disagreeable thoughts.

It is for the consideration of his subjects that the
king has to abide by the law; if not, the king is
above law.

What man makes is the personality of God,
not His reality.

Many evils are born of riches, but many more still
breed in poverty.

The spirit of controversy lives on argument.

Death is preferable to asking favour of a small person.

Let the devil sleep rather than be awake.

A biting tongue goes deeper than the point
of a bayonet.

Cutting words pierce deeper than a poisoned sword.

Human character may be likened to metal;
if you wish to make anything out of metal,
you must melt it. So the human heart must be melted
before it can be made into a desirable character.

The fountain stream of love rises in the love for an
individual, but spreads and falls down in
universal love.

A tender-hearted sinner is better than one who is
hardened by piety.

The way to get over one's error is to admit one's
fault first and then to refrain from falling into it again.

By accusing anyone of his fault,
you only make him firm in it.

When man rises above the limitation of duty,
then duty becomes his pleasure.

When envy develops into jealousy,
the heart turns from sour to bitter.

One who is a riddle to another is a puzzle to himself.

When the miser shows any generosity,
he celebrates it with trumpets.

A sincere man has a fragrance about him
which a sincere heart perceives.

If you are not able to control your thought,
you cannot hold it.

It is the spirit of hopelessness that blocks the path
of man and prevents his advancement.

Sincerity is like a bud in the heart of man,
and it blossoms with the maturity of soul.

No one will experience in life
that which is not meant for him.

It is impossible to be only praised and not be blamed.
Praise and blame go together, hand in hand.

To be in uncongenial surroundings is worse than being
in one's grave.

Science is born of the seed of intuition,
conceived in reason.

Truth alone is success
and the real success is the truth.

When the cry of the disciple has reached a certain pitch,
the Teacher comes to answer it.

People who are difficult to deal with,
are difficult to themselves.

It is sympathy rather than food which will satisfy
your guest.

The man who is not courageous enough to take risks,
will not accomplish anything.

As the flower is the forerunner of the fruit,
so man's childhood is the promise of his life.

Do not offend a low person; it is like throwing a stone
in the mud and getting splashes upon oneself.

The self-made man is greater than the one
who depends on another to make him.

False politeness is like imitation jewelry.

Do not accept that which you cannot return,
for the balance of life is in reciprocity.

Those whom their individuality fails, seek their refuge
in community.

Taking the path of inharmony is like entering
the mouth of the dragon.

Life is an opportunity; it is a great pity that man
realizes this when it is already too late.

Love is the divine Mother's arms; and when those
arms are outspread, every soul falls into them.

The greatest tragedy of the world is the lack
of general evolution.

There is nothing to be surprised at in life;
all situations of life work toward some definite end.

Forgiveness belongs to God; it becomes the privilege
of mortal man only when asked by another.

Every moment of life is a precious moment.

Man learns his first lesson of love by loving a human
being, but in reality love is due to God alone.

You need not look for a saint or a master;
a wise man is sufficient to guide your path.

The man who cannot learn his lesson by his first fault
in life is certainly on the wrong track.

Overlook the greatest fault of another,
but do not partake of it in the smallest degree.

The fulfilment of every activity is in its balance.

The heart of man is a temple; when its door is closed
to man, it is also closed to God.

Success is achieved when free will and circumstances
work hand in hand.

Every impression of a bad happening should be met
with a combative attitude.

Those guilty of the same fault unite in making a virtue
out of their common sin.

Wickedness that manifests from the intelligent person is like a poisonous fruit coming out of a fertile ground.

A joke tickles the intelligence and clears away the clouds of gloom from the heart.

Service of God means we each work for all.

If you wish to probe the depths of a man's character, test him with wine, wealth or woman.

It is the lack of personal magnetism which makes man look for magnetic objects.

Fire can cook food or burn it; so is the effect of pain upon the human heart.

Every desire increases a power by which man can accomplish his main desire, which is the desire of every soul.

Every experience, good or bad, is a step forward in man's evolution in life.

It is no use saying, "I know the truth"; if you knew the truth you would keep silent.

Human suffering is the first call we have to answer.

It is easy to become a teacher, but difficult to become a pupil.

As poison acts as nectar in some cases,
so in certain situations evil proves to be a virtue.

To find apt words to express one's thoughts
is like making a good shot.

He who realizes the effect of his deed upon himself
commences to open his outlook on life.

What man makes God breaks; what God makes
man destroys.

All things are good, but they are not good for every
person nor right for all times.

The false ego is a false god; when the false god
is destroyed, the true God comes.

When a person does not listen to us,
we must know that it comes from this,
that we ourselves do not believe.

The common disease is considered as normal health
by the generality.

Love in its beginning can only live on reciprocity;
but when developed can stand on its own feet.

The present spirit of humanity has commercialism
as its crown and materialism as its throne.

Without humour life is empty.

To see life as a whole is beyond the power
of the generality.

No object or life can exist that has not one central
point in which everything meets and joins together,
and that meeting ground is called the divine mind.

The more you make of your gifts, the less becomes
the value of something which is priceless.

The secret of life is balance, and the absence of
balance is life's destruction.

GAMAKAS.

I consider myself second to none since I have realized
in myself the One Alone.

All things that may seem to be exalting my position,
they indeed lower me in my eyes; the only thing
exalting for me is the forgetting of myself entirely
in the perfect vision of God.

There is nothing that I consider too good for me or
too high to attain to; on the contrary, all possible
attainments seem within my reach since I have
attained to the vision of my Lord.

There is nothing that I feel too humiliated to do, and
there is no position, however exalted, that can make
me feel prouder than what already I am in the pride
of the Lord.

Neither does love exalt nor hate depress me,
for all things to me seem natural.
Life for me is a dream that changeth constantly,
and when I withdraw my real self from the false,
I know all things and yet stand remote;
so I rise above all changes of life.

It makes no difference to me if I am so praised
that I am raised from Earth to Heaven,
or if I am so blamed that I am thrown
from the greatest heights to the depths of the earth;

life to me is an ever-moving sea in which the waves
of favour and disfavour constantly rise and fall.

A fall does not break or discourage me,
it only raises me to a new life.

I could not have enjoyed virtue's beauty
if I had not known sin.

Every loss in life I consider as the throwing off of
an old garment in order to put on a new one; and
the new garment has always been better than
the old one.

I have learned more by my faults than by my merits.
If I acted always aright, then I could not be human.

My intuition never fails me, but I fail whenever I do
not listen to my intuition.

Patience is the lesson I had from the moment
I stepped on the earth; ever since I have tried
to practise it, but more there is to be learnt.

I blame no one for his wrong doing; neither do I
encourage him in that direction.

In bringing happiness to others I feel the pleasure of God,
and for my inadvertence I feel myself blameworthy
before God.

Every soul stands before me as a world, and the light of my spirit falling upon it brings clearly to my view all it contains.

Nothing seems to me either too good or too bad; I know no distinction any more between saint and sinner since I behold the one single life manifested in all.

My action toward every man I consider as my action toward God, and the action of every person toward me I take as an action of God.

As long as I act upon my own intuition I succeed, but whenever I follow the advice of others I go astray.

I work simply, not troubling about results.
My satisfaction is in accomplishing the work
which is given to me to my best ability,
and I leave the effect to the Cause.

Life in the world is most interesting, but the solitude is never enough for me.

I feel myself when I am by myself.

By respecting every person I meet I worship God.

In loving every soul on earth
I feel my devotion to God.

There is nothing else in life which pleases me more
than pleasing others, but it is difficult
to please everybody.

I am ready to learn from those who come to teach me,
and willing to teach those who wish to learn.

I regard every failure as a stepping stone
toward a success.

I will have Heaven or Hell but not Purgatory.

I do not intend to teach my fellowman, but to show
him all I see.

Hail to my exile from the Garden of Eden to the earth;
if I had not fallen, I would not have probed
the depths of life.

At the moment when I shall be leaving this earth,
it is not the number of followers
which will make me proud;
it is the thought that I have delivered His Message
to some souls that will console me,
and the feeling that it helped them through life
that will bring me satisfaction.

I have not come to change humanity,
I have come to help it on.

If anyone throws it down, my heart does not break,
it bursts and the flame coming rises from it,
which becomes my torch.

My deep sigh rises above as a cry of the earth,
and an answer comes from within as a message.

I am a tide in the sea of life, bearing toward the shore
all who come within my enfoldment.

GAYATRI.

Saum.

Praise be to Thee, Most Supreme God,
   Omnipotent, Omnipresent, All-pervading,
   the Only Being.
Take us in Thy Parental Arms,
   raise us from the denseness of the earth,
   Thy Beauty do we worship,
   to Thee do we give willing surrender.
Most Merciful and Compassionate God,
   the Idealized Lord of the whole humanity,
   Thee only do we worship,
   and towards Thee Alone we aspire.
Open our hearts towards Thy Beauty,
   illuminate our souls with Divine Light,
   O Thou, the Perfection of Love, Harmony and
      Beauty,
   All-powerful Creator, Sustainer,
   Judge and Forgiver of our shortcomings,
   Lord God of the East and of the West,
   of the worlds above and below,
   and of the seen and unseen beings:
Pour upon us Thy Love and Thy Light,
   give sustenance to our bodies, hearts and souls,
   use us for the purpose that Thy Wisdom chooseth,
   and guide us on the path of Thine Own Goodness.
Draw us closer to Thee every moment of our life,
   until in us be reflected Thy Grace,
   Thy Glory, Thy Wisdom, Thy Joy and Thy Peace.
                                        Amen.

Salat.

Most Gracious Lord,
   Master, Messiah and Saviour of humanity,
   we greet Thee with all humility.
Thou art the First Cause and the Last Effect,
   the Divine Light and the Spirit of Guidance,
   Alpha and Omega.
Thy Light is in all forms, Thy Love in all beings:
   in a loving mother , in a kind father,
   in an innocent child, in a helpful friend
   and in an inspiring teacher.
Allow us to recognize Thee
   in all Thy Holy Names and Forms:
   as Rama, as Krishna, as Shiva, as Buddha;
   let us know Thee as Abraham, as Solomon,
   as Zarathushtra, as Moses, as Jesus,
      as Muhammad,
   and in many more Names and Forms,
   known and unknown to the world.
We adore Thy Past,
   Thy Presence deeply enlightens our being,
   and we look for Thy Blessing in the future,
   O Messenger, Christ, Nabi, the Rasul of God.
Thou whose heart constantly reacheth upwards,
   thou comest on earth with a Message,
   as a dove from above when dharma decayeth,
   and speakest the Word that is put into thy mouth,
   as the light filleth the crescent moon.
Let the star of the Divine Light shining in thy heart
   be reflected in the hearts of thy devotees.

May the Message of God reach far and wide,
   illuminating and making the whole humanity
   as one single brotherhood in the Fatherhood
      of God.

Amen.

Khatm.

O Thou, Who art the Perfection
   of Love, Harmony and Beauty,
      the Lord of the Heaven and the earth,
Open our hearts, that we may hear Thy Voice,
   Which constantly cometh from within.
Disclose to us Thy Divine Light,
   Which is hidden in our souls,
      that we may know and understand life better.
Most Merciful and Compassionate God,
   give us Thy Great Goodness,
   teach us Thy Loving Forgiveness,
   raise us above the distinctions
   and differences which divide men,
   send us the Peace of Thy Divine Spirit,
   and unite us all in Thy Perfect Being.

Amen.

Dowa.

Save me, my Lord,
   from the earthly passions
   and the attachments which blind mankind.
Save me, my Lord,
   from the temptations of power, fame and wealth,
   which keep man away from Thy Glorious Vision.

47

Save me, my Lord,
  from the souls who are constantly occupied
  in hurting and harming their fellow-man,
  and who take pleasure in the pain of another.
Save me, my Lord,
  from the evil eye of envy and jealousy,
  which falleth upon Thy Bountiful Gifts.
Save me, my Lord,
  from falling into the hands
  of the playful children of earth;
  they might use me in their games;
  they might play with me and then break me
  in the end, as children destroy their toys.
Save me, my Lord,
  from all manner of injury that cometh
  from the bitterness of my adversaries
  and from the ignorance of my loving friends.
                                        Amen.

Nayaz.

Beloved Lord, Almighty God,
through the rays of the sun,
through the waves of the air,
through the all-pervading life in space,
purify and revivify me, and I pray,
heal my body, heart and soul.

                                        Amen.

Nazr.

O Thou,
the Sustainer of our bodies, hearts and souls,
bless all that we receive in thankfulness.
                                        Amen.

48

RAGAS.

Thy Light hath illuminated the dark chamber
   of my mind;
Thy Love is rooted in the depth of my heart.
Thine Ears are attached to my heart;
Thine Eyes are the sight of my soul.
Thy Power works behind my action;
Thy Peace is alone the repose in my life.
Thy Will works behind my every impulse;
Thy Voice speaketh my words.
Thine own image is my countenance;
My body covereth Thy Soul.
My life is Thy very Breath, my Beloved;
And my self is Thine own Being.

Thou pourest wine into my empty cup
   wherever we meet,
   on hills and dales,
   on the top of the high mountains,
   in the thick forests,
   and in the barren deserts,
   on the shores of the roaring sea,
   and on the banks of the gentle river,
And there arise in my heart
   the unearthly passion and the heavenly joy.

Thou hast won my heart
   a thousand times over again.
Thou comest veiled
   under many and varied guises
   and in every guise Thou art unique.

Who is not deluded by the splendour
   Thou hast so skilfully produced
   on the face of the earth?
In this beauty fair Thou shinest,
   adorned in myriad garbs.
Thine own is all the beauty
   and it is Thou Thyself
   Who art attracted by it.
Thou on the stage of life
   actest as friend, as foe,
   and Thou alone seest this play
   performed so wonderfully.
I sought Thee so long, my Beloved,
   and now I have found Thee at last,
   O Winner of my heart,
And in finding Thee I have lost myself.

Let me feel Thine Arms around me, Beloved,
   while I am wandering away from home.
Let my heart become Thy lute.
   Hearing Thy song my soul cometh to life.
Let my virgin soul dance at Thy court, my Indra,
   the passion it hath is for Thee alone.
O let me lean my head on Thy Breast,
   Thine Arms enfolding me,
   my feet touch Paradise.

Wherever I see, I see Thy beloved Face
   covered under many different veils.
The magic power of my everseeking eyes
   lifted the veil from Thy glowing countenance,

And Thy sweet smiles win my heart
   a thousand times over.
The lustre of Thy piercing glance
   has lighted my darkened soul,
And lo, now I see the sun shine everywhere.

On the bright sunny day
   and in the darkness of night,
     what didst Thou not teach me!
Thou hast taught me what is meant by wrong
   and what is called right.
Thou hast shown me the hideous face of life
   and Thou hast unveiled before me
     life's beautiful countenance.
Thou hast taught me wisdom
   out of utter darkness of ignorance.
Thou hast taught me to think
   after my thoughtless hours
And Thou playest with me,
   my Beloved Lord, my Master,
     hide and seek.
Thou didst close my eyes
   and Thou hast opened them.

When we are face to face, Beloved,
   I do not know
     whether to call Thee me, or me Thee.
I see my self when Thou art not before me;
   when I see Thee, my self is lost to my view.
I consider it a great fortune
   when Thou art alone with me,

but when I am not at all there,
I think it the greatest luck.

Thy whispering to the ears of my heart
  moveth my soul to ecstasy.
The waves of joy that rise in my heart
  make a swing for Thy living word.
My heart passionately awaiteth Thy word,
  deaf to all that calleth from without.
Thou Who art enshrined in my heart,
  speak some more;
    Thy voice exalteth my soul.

When Thou art before me, my Beloved,
  I rise upon wings
  and my burden becometh light;
But when my little self riseth before my eyes,
  I drop to the earth
  and all its weight falleth upon me.

My soul is moved to dance
  by the charm of Thy graceful movements,
And my heart beateth the rhythm
  of Thy gentle steps.
The sweet impression of Thy winning countenance,
  my worshipped One,
  co
vereth all visible things from my sight.
My heart re-echoes the melody
  Thou playest on Thy flute.
And it bringeth my soul in harmony
  with the whole universe.

I dare not think of raising my eyes
    to look at Thy glorious vision.
I quietly sit by the lake of my heart,
    watching in it Thy most lovely image
    reflected.

Thou givest me Thine own Love
    and Thou winnest my heart
    with the charm of Thy Beauty.
When I approach Thee fondly, my Beloved,
    Thou sayest to me: "Touch me not!"

I cling to Thee with a child's faith,
    bearing in my heart Thy most lovely image.
I have sought refuge under Thy bosom, Beloved,
    and I am safe, feeling Thine arms around me.

How shall I thank Thee, my King,
    for Thy bountiful gifts?
Every gift Thou givest me, my generous Lord,
    is invaluable.
A tongue of flame arose
    out of the twinkling spark of my heart
    by Thy gentle blowing.
Thou hast opened the ears of my heart
    that I may hear Thy softest whisper.
Thou hast taught me Thine own tongue
    and to read the characters written by Thy pen.

I call Thee my King when I am conscious
    of my bubble-like self,
But when I am conscious of Thee, my Beloved,
    I call Thee me.

How shall I thank Thee
    for Thy mercy and compassion,
    O King of my soul?
What didst Thou not do unto me?
When I was walking alone through the wilderness,
    through the darkness of night,
    Thou didst come with Thy lighted torch
    and didst illuminate my path.
Frozen with the coldness
    of the world's hardness of heart
    I sought refuge in Thee
    and Thou didst console me
    with Thine endless love.
I knocked at Thy gate at last,
    when I had no answer
    from anywhere in the world,
and Thou didst answer readily
    my broken heart's call.

I searched and searched and searched
    and I could not find Thee anywhere.
I called Thee aloud, standing on the minaret.
I rang the temple bell
    with the rising and setting of the sun.
I bathed in the Ganges in vain.
I came back from Ka'ba disappointed;

I looked for Thee in heaven,
  my Beloved, my Pearl,
but at last I have found Thee
  hidden in the shell of my heart.

I would willingly die a thousand deaths,
  if by dying I could attain
  Thy most lofty presence.
If a cup of poison Thy lovely hands offered,
  I would prefer that poison
  to the bowl of nectar.
I value the dust under Thy feet, my Precious One,
  most of all the treasures the earth holds.
If my head could touch the earth
  of Thy dwelling place,
  I would proudly refuse Khusrou's crown.
I would gladly sacrifice all pleasures
  the earth can offer me,
  if I could only retain the pain
  I have in my feeling heart.

One moment's life lived with Thee
  is worth more than a life of long years
  lived in Thine absence.

Give me one more cup, O Saqi,
  which I will value more
  than the whole life I have lived.

My lifelong sorrow I forget
  when Thou casteth one glance o'er me;

Time is not for me, a glimpse of Thy glorious
    vision maketh me eternal.

It is Thou Who art my pride;
    When I realize my limited self,
    I feel humblest of all living beings.

O Thou, the root of my life's plant,
    Thou wert hidden so long
    in my bud-like soul.
But now Thou hast come out,
    O my life's fruit,
    after the blossoming of my heart.

Let me grow quietly in Thy garden
    as a speechless plant,
that some day my flowers and fruits
    might sing the legend of my silent past.

Thy music causeth my soul to dance.
In the cooing of the wind
    I hear Thy trumpet,
and through the gentle breeze
    cometh to my ears
    the music of Thy flute.
The waves in the sea
    keep the rhythm of my dancing steps.
In the noise of the thunder
    I hear Thy drums,
and the lightning playeth to me
    the music of cymbals.

Through the whole nature
   I hear Thy music played,
   my Beloved,
and my soul while dancing,
   speaketh of its joy in song.

Thy smiling eyes have brought
   my dead heart to life again;
My life and death depend
   upon the closing and disclosing
   of Thy magic glance.

SURAS.

Blessed is he
  who has found in his life his life's purpose.
Blessed is he
  who resteth in the abode of his soul.
Blessed is he
  who heareth the call
  from the minaret of his heart.
Blessed is he
  who seeth the star of his soul
  as the light seen from the sea.

Blessed are the innocent
  who believe and trust simply.

Blessed are the unselfish friends
  whose motto in life is constancy.

Blessed are they
  who strive in the path of Truth patiently.

Blessed are they
  who make willing sacrifices in kindness.

Blessed are they
  who cover the holes of others
  even from their own eyes.

Blessed are they
  who fear that they might hurt another
  by their thought or word or deed.

Blessed are the proud in God,
   for they shall inherit the Kingdom of Heaven.

Verily the heart
   that reflecteth the divine Light
   is illuminated.
Verily the heart
   that is respondent to the divine Word
   is liberated.
Verily the heart
   that receiveth the divine Peace
   is blessed.
Verily the heart
   that repeateth the sacred Name
   is exalted.
Verily the heart
   that cherisheth the love of God
   will be crowned with the divine glory
   on the last day.

Enviable is he who loveth
   and asketh for no return.

It is truth that every soul is seeking.

Verily he is victorious
   who has conquered himself.

Life is one continual battle,
   and he who will conquer himself
   will alone gain victory over it.

Verily all that leads to happiness is good.

Verily he is pious who considers human feeling.

For every unfoldment there is a certain time,
  so there comes a time
  for the unfoldment of the soul.

The period of one's spiritual development
  depends upon the rhythm of one's life.

All things which one seeks in God,
  such as light, life, strength, joy and peace,
  these all can be found in Truth.
Verily God is Truth.

Truth is the light
  which illuminates the whole life.

Truth is the evidence of God,
  and God is the evidence of Truth.

In the light of Truth all things become clear,
  their true nature manifests to view.

When man closes his lips, God begins to speak.

There is no Teacher save God;
  we all learn from Him.

The consciousness of the one whole
  is the flesh of Christ
  and the breath of love is his blood.

60

If the Almighty God chooseth
   He hath power sufficient
   to turn thy shield
   into a poisoned sword
   and even thine own hand
   into the arm of thine adversary.

Your great enemies are those
   who are near and dear to you,
But your still greater enemy
   is your own self.

Out of space arose light,
   and by that light space became illuminated.

Put your trust in God for support,
   and see His hidden Hand
   working through all sources.

Man looks for wonders;
   if he only saw how very wonderful
   is the heart of man.

Do not cry with the crying ones,
   but console them;
   if not, by your sympathy
   you will make them cry more.

One word can be more precious
   than all the treasures of the earth.

He who maketh room in the heart
   will find accommodation everywhere.

External life
   is but the shadow of the inner reality.

The secret of all success
   is the strength of conviction.

Those who try to make virtues
   out of their faults,
   grope further and further into the darkness.

Patient endurance is the sign of progress.

Do not fear God, but regard carefully
   His pleasure and displeasure.

Temptation is that which detains one
   on his journey to the desired goal.

Fatality is one side of the Truth, not all.

O righteous one, keep your goodness distant
   that it may not touch your sense of vanity.

The great teachers of humanity
   become streams of love.

He whose love has been reciprocated
   has not known what is love.

Faith assures success.

The key to all happiness is the love of God.

As the shadow is apparent
   and yet non-existent,
   so is evil.

To know the justice of God
   you must be just yourself.

To whom the soul truly belongs,
   to Him in the end it returns.

In order to realize perfection
   man must lose his imperfect self
   in the perfection of God.

The hereafter is the continuity
   of the same life in another sphere.

Those who live with God
   look to Him for guidance
   at every move they make.

Independence and indifference
   are as two wings
   which enable the soul to fly.

Resignation is no good,
   except in cases where a thing is done
   and it can't be helped.

Learn to live a true life
and you will know the truth.

The world itself becomes a scripture or book
to the soul.

He is an unbeliever
who cannot believe himself.

A pure life and clear conscience
are as two eyes for the soul.

Righteousness comes from the essence
of every soul.

When man's self does not belong to him,
what else can belong to him?

There is no source of happiness
other than the heart of man.

Faithfulness has a fragrance to it
which is perceived in the atmosphere
of the faithful.

One who does not recognize God,
sooner or later God will make him
recognize Him.

As soon as you knock at the gate of God,
which is your heart,
from there the answer comes.

There is no greater phenomenon
   than love itself.

While life is full of blessings,
   we only must know how to be blessed by it.

Where the body goes,
   there the shadow will go also.
So is Truth followed by falsehood.

Life in the world is false,
   and its lovers revel in falsehood.

Faith means a living trust.

Faith in self
   must culminate into faith in God.

The sun-glass reflects the heart of the sun;
   the contemplative heart
   reflects the divine qualities.

The soul is either raised or cast down
   by the power of its own thoughts,
   speech and action.

Every soul seeks after beauty,
   and every virtue, righteousness, good action
   is nothing but a glimpse of beauty.

To be alone by oneself
   is like being with a friend,
   whose company will last for ever.

It is the tongue of flame
  which speaketh the truth,
  not the tongue of flesh.

He to whom his life's purpose is clear
  is already on the path.

All which is precious we naturally hide;
  so the truth is hidden
  in the heart of nature.

We give a way to our faults
  by being passive to them.

The more a man explores himself,
  the more power he finds within himself,
  which he could never have realized
  otherwise.

The ideal is the flower of the creation
  and the realization of Truth
  is its fragrance.

The secret of the whole creation
  is the hidden desire of the Creator.

The Soul of Christ
  is the life of the universe.

The possessor of wealth
  is often a gate-keeper of his treasure house.

The words that enlighten
   are more precious than jewels.

Faith reaches what reason fails to touch.

The whole world's treasure
   is too small a price
   for a word that kindles the soul.

Of what use is your sense, O sensible one,
   if it come to mourn
   over the opportunity you have lost.

If you will fail yourself,
   everybody will fail you.

If you are the master of your own domain,
   you certainly are the king of the world.

Means sufficient for the need
   of everyday simple life
   are a greater boon than the riches
   that add to life's struggle.

In order to bring ourselves
   up to our ideal,
   first we must realize our own follies,
   next we must try to become better,
   believing that we can change.

67

When it is difficult
   even for the worldly people
   to live in the world,
   how much more difficult
   must it be for the Godly.

When man has to choose
   between his spiritual and material profit,
   then he shows whether his treasure is on earth
   or in heaven.

Love is inexpressible in its fulness,
   but it is a power
   that speaks louder than words.

There is nothing that man is too weak to do
   when love's power gushes forth
   from his heart.

Spiritual attainment
   is tuning oneself to a high pitch.

Unless you respect your own ideal
   others will not respect it.

Believe in your own ideal first
   if you wish others to believe it.

The man who will attain power,
   not knowing its proper use,
   will lose it in the end
   with a considerable loss.

Power most often costs more than it is worth.

All that is held under power
   must some day revolt.

Man shows himself to be greater or smaller
   according to the importance he attaches
   to greater or smaller things in life.

There is nothing on earth or in Heaven
   which is not in the reach of man.
When God is in his reach,
   what else could be out of his reach?

In faith is the secret of fulfilment
   or non-fulfilment of every thought.

Self-confidence is the true meaning of faith.

There is a limit to the precautions
   one takes in one's life's affairs,
   and that limit is trust in God.

The one who walks regardless of success,
   success pursues him.
The one who pursues success in life,
   success runs before him.

Some are masters of success and some slaves.

There are two kinds among the seekers of God;
   one makes Him and the other mars.

Every thought, speech and action
   which is natural, sound and living
   is a virtue;
   and that which lacks the same
   is sin.

TALAS.

Silence serves
    as a lock on the lips of the excitable;
    as a barrier between two hearts
    severed from one another;
    as a shield for the wise amidst fools;
    as a veil over the face of the unlettered
    before the well-versed folks.

Love from above is forgiveness.
Love from below is devotion.
Love from within is kindness,
    and love from without is affection.

One who returns more good for less good
    is a good man.
One who returns less good for more good
    is selfish.
One who tries to be even
    in the exchange of good
    is a practical person.
But the one who returns good for evil
    is a saint.

One who returns less evil for more evil
    is ordinary.
One who tries to be even in returning evil
    is wicked.
One who returns more evil for less evil
    is cruel.
But the one who returns evil for good,
    for him there is no name.

He who guards himself
   against being fooled by another
   is clever;
he who does not allow another to fool him
   is wise;
he who is fooled by another
   is a simpleton,
but he who knowingly allows himself
   to be fooled
   shows the character of the saint.

If you wish people to obey you,
   you must learn to obey yourself.
If you wish people to believe you,
   you must learn to believe yourself.
If you wish people to respect you.
   you must learn to respect yourself.
If you wish people to trust you.
   you must learn to trust yourself.

Man proves to be genuine by his sincerity.
Man proves to be noble
   by his charity of heart.
Man proves to be wise by his tolerance,
   and man proves to be great by his endurance
   through the constantly jarring influences
   of life.

He is brave
   who courageously experiences all things.
He is a coward
   who is afraid to take a step
   in a new direction.

He is foolish
   who swims with tides of fancy and pleasure.
He is wise
   who experiences all things,
   yet keeps on the path
   that leads him to his destination.

The warder of the prison
   is in a worse position
   than the prisoner himself;
while the body of the prisoner
   is in captivity,
the mind of the warder is in prison.

For all you take in this world
   you must pay a price;
   for some things you must pay in advance,
   for some things you should pay on delivery,
   and for some later,
   when you receive the bill.
Life is a fair trade;
   all adjusts itself therein in its own time.

Master is he who masters self.
Teacher is he who teaches self.
Governor is he who governs self,
and ruler is he who rules self.

He who is frightened of the vice
   is subject to the vice.
He who is addicted to the vice
   is its captive.

He who acquaints himself with the vice
   is the pupil of the vice,
   he learns his lesson from it.
But he who passeth through vice
   and riseth above it
   is master and conqueror.

The simpleton eats more
   than he can assimilate.
The simpleton collects more load
   than he can carry.
The simpleton cuts the same branch
   of the tree on which he sits.
The simpleton spreads thorns
   in his own path.

The one who says, "I cannot tolerate"
   shows his smallness.
The one who says, "I cannot endure"
   shows his weakness.
The one who says, "I cannot associate"
   shows his limitation.
The one who says, "I cannot forgive"
   shows his imperfection.

Who has failed himself, has failed all,
Who has conquered himself, has won all.

Happy is he
   who does good to others,
And miserable is he
   who expects good from others.

Love that is progressive
   is like the sweet water
   of the running river,
But love that doth not progress
   is like the salt water of the sea.

It is wicked to pick holes in people;
It is clever to see through subtle ways;
It is foolish to be taken in by people;
It is wise to see all things
   and overlook them.

Man creates his death;
   if not so, he was born to live.

Life is a captivity;
   death is the relief from it.

Belief in God is the fuel,
Love of God is the glow,
And the realization of God
   is the flame of divine light.

The first birth is the birth of man,
The next birth is the birth of God.

What Brahma creates in a year,
   Vishnu enjoys for a day,
   and Shiva destroys it in a moment.

Success leads to success,
   and failure follows a failure.

It is simple to tie a knot of attachment,
   but it is difficult when you wish
   to unravel it.

Good praises good; bad fights bad.

The difference between war and peace
   is that war is using sword against another
   and peace is using sword toward oneself.

Fight against the enemy means war.
Fight against oneself means peace.

Snakes breed under a throne
   and scorpions under a crown.

If you are subtle and intelligent,
   that is natural;
But if you are simple and wise,
   you are a mystery.

We must forget the past,
   manage the present
   and prepare the future.

Mountains can be broken through,
   the ocean can be crossed,
   a way may be made through the air;
But you cannot find a way to work
   with a person who is hardened
   in his character,
   deep-set in his ideas,
   and fixed in his outlook on life.

What science cannot declare, art can suggest.
What art suggests silently, poetry speaks out.
But what poetry fails to explain in words
   is expressed by music.

He who does not lose the opportunity
   of doing some good in life is good,
And he who seizes upon such an opportunity
   when it occurs is better still;
But he who always looks out
   for an opportunity to bring some good
   is best among men.

He who appeals to the human intellect
   will knock at the gate of the human brain,
   he is a speaker;
He who appeals to the human emotions
   will enter into the hearts of men,
   he is a preacher;
But he who penetrates the spirit
   of his hearers
   is the prophet,
   who will abide in their souls for ever.

Passion is the smoke
   and emotion is the glow of love's fire;
Selflessness is the flame
   that illuminates the path.

He who has spent has used;
He who has collected has lost;
But he who has given
   has saved his treasure for ever.

He who knows not the truth is a child;
He who is seeking truth is a youth;
But he who has found truth is an old soul.

Be contented with what you possess in life;
Be thankful for what does not belong to you,
   for it is so much care the less,
But try to obtain what you need in life,
   and make the best of every moment
   of your life.

The rock can be cut and polished,
   hard metal can be melted and moulded;
But the mind of the foolish person
   is most difficult to work with.

From the body of love comes reciprocity;
From the heart of love comes beneficence;
But from the soul of love
   is born renunciation.

Make your heart as soft as wax
   to sympathize with others,
But make it as hard as a rock
   to bear the hard knocks of the world.

The path of freedom
   does not lead to the goal of freedom;
It is the path of discipline
   which leads to the goal of liberty.

Present is the reflection of the past,
   and future is the re-echo
   of the present.

Strength increases strength,
   and weakness brings a greater weakness.

Translation is a reincarnation,
   and interpretation is transmigration
   of an idea.

His worry is in vain
   who thinks why others are not
   what they ought to be,
But the one who asks why he is not
   what he ought to be is wise.

One who fights his nature for his ideal
   is a saint;
One who subjects his ideal to his realization
   of truth
   is the master.

To an angelic soul
   love means glorification;
To a jinn soul
   love means admiration;
To a human soul
   love means affection;
To an animal soul
   love means passion.

He is living whose sympathy is awake,
    and he is dead whose heart is asleep.

What you create blindly
    your intelligence destroys,
And what your wisdom creates
    is destroyed by your ignorance.

Man is his own example;
    if he be false, all is false to him,
    and if he be true, all is true to him.

Whichever path you choose to tread,
    the right or the wrong,
There is at the back always a powerful hand
    to push you along.

Who can live up to his ideal
    is the king of life;
And who cannot live up to it
    is its slave.

When man denies what he owes you,
    then it is put on the account of God.

The unselfish profits by life
    more than the selfish one,
    whose profit in the end
    proves to be a loss.

Among a million believers in God
    there is scarcely one
    who maketh God a reality.

If you live in the vision of the past,
    dream on,
    do not open your eyes to the present.
If you live in the eternal now, go on,
    do not trouble about the morrow.
But if you live for the time to come,
    do all you can to prepare the future.

It is better to refuse
    than to accept anything unwillingly.

There is no end to reproaches in one's life,
    not only those at a distance and those
    near to one, but even the members of one's
    body will some day reproach one for not
    having received proper care and full
    attention.

The man who holds the world
    is vaster than the world,
And whom the world holds is small.

There is as much likeness
    between falsehood and truth
    as there is between the person
    and his shadow,
    the difference being that while
    the former has life, the latter has none.

When man rises above the earth,
    the earth is at his feet;
But when he falls beneath the earth,
    the earth is over his head.

TANAS.

Sundew, why is it that every insect
   that kisses you dies instantly?
I like him so much that I eat him up.

Sundew, where did you learn this moral?
   A voice said to me
   "I am the love and I am the life,
   and whoever cometh to me,
   by one embrace I turn him into my own life".

Celandines, what do you signify?
We are the lights of the earth.

Rosebud, what were you doing at night?
I was praying to Heaven with closed hands
   to open my heart.

Waterlily, what do you represent
   by your white garland?
The purity of the heart of this lake.

Tulip, why have you opened your lips?
To tell you what I have learnt in silence.

What did you learn?
To make of oneself an empty cup.

Orchid, what do your petals represent?
Graceful movements of dance.

What does your dance express?
The earth paying homage to Heaven.

Little daisies,
   why do you keep so close to the earth?
Because earth is the home
   of all mortal beings

Little daisies,
   what gospel do you read?
Blessed are the meek,
   for they shall inherit the earth.

Little daisies,
   what are you here for?
To represent Heaven on earth.

Little daisies,
   what is your daily duty?
To console the hearts which are trodden upon.

Little daisies,
   what are you doing here in the churchyard?
We worship God by bowing at the feet
   of His creatures.

Cactus, why are you fringed with thorns?
I am the tongue of the malicious man.

Cactus, why is your stem so thorny?
I am the hand of the evil-doer.

Cactus, why have you thorns on your leaf?
I am the heart of the wicked
   who take pleasure in hurting others.

Beautiful gorses, what are you?
We are little lanterns on your path.

But where do you get your prickly thorns?
Flowers from above and thorns from below.

Roseplant, what are you? Friend or foe?
I am both. I have my flowers and thorns.

Wheatgrains, why do you grow
    so close together?
Unity is our strength,
    that is why you seek in us
    your life's subsistence.

Palm-tree,
    what do your outstretched hands signify?
I raise hands heavenward when I pray,
    then pass the blessing on to the earth.

Fir-trees, what are you?
We are the souls of the sages
    who preferred vigil in the solitude
    to the busy life of the world.

Fir-trees, what are you?
We are hands from heaven, stretched out
    to bless the earth continually.

Fir-trees, what are you made for?
We are the temples
    made for those who worship God in nature.

Fir-trees, what are you doing in this forest?
We are the souls on the cross,
    patiently awaiting
    the hour of our liberation.

Dry wood, why do they burn you?
Because I no longer can bear fruit.

Thunderstorm, what arouses your passion?
The beauty of the earth.

Full moon, where will you be going from here?
Into retreat.

Why do you take a retreat after your fulness?
To make myself an empty cup
    in order to rise again.

Church bell, what do you call out?
Every head that resounds like me,
    it spreads abroad the Message of God.

Church bell, what do you repeat?
The sacred name of God
    which resounds through my whole being.

Church bell, what makes you move?
The word of God.

Incense, what do you teach at the church?
He who endureth pain for the cause of others
  must rise from the mortal world
  to the spheres of immortality.

Incense, what were you whispering
  at the church service?
No prayer can reach God
  unless it arises from a glowing heart.

Incense, what does your scent signify?
My scent is the evidence of my self-sacrifice.

Incense, tell me the secret of your self.
I am the feeling heart of the lover,
  whose deep sigh rises upwards,
  spreading its perfume all around.

Incense, tell me what moral
  is veiled in your nature.
When my heart endures the test of fire,
  my hidden quality becomes manifest.

Coin, what are you?
I am the seal of hearts.
  A heart once sealed by me
  will love no one but me.

Money, when you leave,
  what becomes of your lover?
I leave behind a mark on my lover's heart
  which always remains as a wound.

Money, what do you like the most?
Changing hands.

Money, which is your dwelling place?
The heart of my worshipper.

Money, where do you accumulate?
Where I am warmly welcomed.

Money, where do you stay?
Where I am worshipped.

Money, whom do you seek?
Who seeks after me.

Money, whom do you worship?
Who is risen above me,
    I become his slave
    and live as dust at his feet.

Devil, where do you find your location?
In doubting eyes, in a sharp tongue,
    in a gossiping mouth,
    in inquisitive ears,
    in idle hands, in restless feet,
    in a vicious body, in a crooked mind,
    in a bitter heart,
    and in a darkened soul.

Devil, how do you express yourself?
In winking eyes, in sneering smiles,
    in cutting words
    and in false tears.

Why, I have no answer for you.
Why, the proper answer for you is: Why?
Why, you are yourself the cover
    over the answer you want.

Why, what a pity you are blind.
Why, what are you?
  I am the cry of the hungry mind.
Why, what do you signify?
  I am the knocker upon the closed door
  to which I am attached.
Why, what do you represent?
  The owl who cannot see during the day.
Why, what is your complaint?
  I am the irritation of mind.
Why, what is your life's condition?
  I am shut up in a dark room.
Why, how long will your captivity last?
  All night long.
Why, what are you so eagerly waiting for?
  The daybreak.
Match-stick,
  what did you say when I struck you?
Why?

My moods, what are you?
We are the waves rising in your heart.

Emotion, where do you come from?
From the ever-running spring of the heart.

Imagination, what are you?
I am the fountain-stream
  that rises from the mind.

88